Signs of the Times

a portrait of the nation's tastes

photographs by Martin Parr
text by Nicholas Barker

CORNERHOUSE PUBLICATIONS

First published in 1992 by
Cornerhouse Publications
70 Oxford Street
Manchester, M1 5NH
061 228 7621

ISBN 0948797 91 6

Design by Alan Ward
Production by Wordsmith, Manchester
Colour prints by Peter Fraser
Printed by Jackson Wilson

In view of the contents of this book it seems only fair that I briefly describe my own taste; for that is what my BBC production team has spent the past eighteen months asking the British public to do.

My taste is, without doubt, contradictory. In some respects it bears the familiar hallmarks of a conventional public school/upper middle class background: I prize qualities such as craftsmanship, authenticity, and rarity, and look with disapproval on tastes which I consider conspicuous, ill-informed, pretentious and unauthentic. In other respects I am happy to abandon discretion in favour of the brash and the absurd. I put this down to a rebellious streak in my character, and a surfeit of James Bond films during my formative years. I would also have to confess to being something of a fashion victim – a fact which rather embarrasses me. Though I would never admit it publicly, I feel I have rather superior taste.

Describing one's taste is by no means easy. It necessarily involves the disclosure of highly personal, potentially embarrassing information which may irritate others and expose oneself to public ridicule. It also begs the question: does the person describing his taste see himself as others do.

The complexities of personal taste in the home are the subject of these photographs by Martin Parr and the television series, SIGNS OF THE TIMES, which they accompany.

Research for the series began in the spring of 1990 and continued until the autumn of 1991. Advertisements were placed regularly with Ceefax and in the national and local press appealing to members of the public to volunteer information about all aspects of their taste in the home. Initially, these appeals had only limited success. It is a truism in television research that people who want to be filmed are often less interesting than people who don't. However respondents frequently put us onto their friends, neighbours and relatives, among whom fruitful contacts were made.

SIGNS OF THE TIMES makes no claims to being a scientific survey of taste in the British home, nor does it advance a theory of personal taste. The 80 or so people featured in the films were selected from 2,000 interviewed nationwide, and are presented without commentary. They represent, in my view, a broad cross-section of contemporary taste selected according to a wide range of criteria, foremost of which were lifestage, gender, ethnicity, social class, region and personality type. No system of quotas was introduced - some people may be cross about this - and every household chosen had to be deemed both *interesting* in the opinion of the production team, as well as representative of some broader issue or trend. Of the 50 households we filmed, Martin Parr photographed 30 having first viewed our film rushes and transcripts of the interviews.

Television documentaries about *real people* have a tendency to select people who represent either a social problem or some quaint aspect of modern life. In either case the editorial objective is to evoke public concern or a pleasant sentimental glow. Commonly assisted by colourful characters who communicate

with ease in a documentary format, the net effect is often to reassure viewers that they are unlike those who have been filmed.

SIGNS OF THE TIMES went in search of neither social problems nor whimsy. Film narrative permitting, it set out to record as objectively as possible a wide range of contemporary tastes, and to present them so that viewers could judge them for themselves. Ordinary and unexceptional tastes were generally chosen in preference to the exotic, and we were gratified by the frequency with which people enquired 'why are you filming us? We're not that different, are we?'

The films and this collection of still photographs are undoubtedly voyeuristic. However, their objective was to transcend mere visual pleasure and establish a sense of complicity between viewers and the people they were invited to gaze upon. The value of this work, such as it is, lies in the quality of its observations and the reflections about personal taste which it stimulates.

Although SIGNS OF THE TIMES refrains from adopting a *position* on personal taste - it rejects the view that there is a quantifiable hierarchy of tastes - if pressed, I would have to concede a personal value judgment: namely all social classes, my own included, display a certain absurdity in their efforts to distinguish themselves from each other.

There's nobody that's ever come in and said, 'Oh I don't like the way you've got the place'

When asked about their tastes, it is striking how

infrequently people refer to strictly aesthetic matters. Instead their choices appear to be governed by a complex mix of public and private concerns: sentimentality, fantasy, personal belief, awareness of age and gender, susceptibility to fashion, and an often shifting self-image, combine with more public anxieties about class, social status and the approval of peers.

To understand why someone favours a striped duvet cover over a flowery one, or a pine mug-tree over a row of hooks, one must first negotiate this intricate maze of feelings and associations for it is only in its totality that an individual's personal taste begins to make sense.

I don't like Austrian blinds. I think they look nice but they're so common Everybody has got them

The SIGNS OF THE TIMES production office is lined with shelves bearing hundreds of taped interviews. Play one at random, and within minutes you will hear people talking about tastes which they find unacceptable or offensive. Most people, it seems, define their taste in opposition to the tastes of others and find it easier to talk about what is wrong with other people's choices rather than what is right about their own. Particularly noteworthy is the way people are quickest to distance themselves from tastes which are both similar to their own and held by others with whom they are competing in some respect. This might account for the way people in my profession save their most venomous criticism for television programmes which are similar to ones they themselves have made.

It would seem that a function of taste is not merely to express difference but to express difference from something in particular - in fact the more specific the better.

There's no way I am gonna go normal and wear old fashioned dresses I'm gonna stay the same and have my nose pierced

The context in which taste is exercised has important bearing on the taste that is actually selected. The landmarks in the evolution of an individual's taste are provided by certain key lifestages such as marriage, the arrival of children, their later departure, divorce - if it applies - and retirement. Each of these stages provides an opportunity for a re-evaluation of one's taste, and adjustments generally follow.

Teenage years, for example, provide the first major occasion for the expression of individuality and difference. Teenage dress codes are invariably adopted in opposition to parental taste as well as the class values it enshrines. However this rebellion is usually short-lived. With each successive change of home, there is often a gradual reversion to the basics of parental taste unless social mobility, cultural assimilation or other such changes cause a lasting rupture with the past.

My tastes are undoubtedly masculine I am not fond of ornamentation or frippery of any kind

A fundamental difference expressed through taste is gender. And the overwhelming majority of men and women whom we interviewed revealed taste preferences which conformed to a wide range of gender stereotypes. In interview after interview, women described how their tastes in the home centred around concerns such as comfort, homeliness, co-ordination, ornamentation, sentimentality and fantasy. Men on the other hand, - particularly the under 40s - seemed eager to conceal evidence of personal emotion, were irritated by all but the largest of ornaments, were embarrassed by excessive decoration - particularly floral designs - and preferred instead to be surrounded by things which they considered *visually impressive*. The patterns they chose were generally *simple but striking*, and their favourite colours were repeatedly shown to be white, black, red and grey.

We are going to come to a nice compromise on every issue. I've decided what colours we're going to have He can just pick the variations

It is one thing to decide upon the taste and the self-image one wishes to project; it is quite another to implement it without the interference of others. With the exception of people who live on their own - they can generally decide for themselves which influences to accept and which to reject - everyone else must cope with the competing pressures of children, flat-mates, spouses and relatives. After a decade in which much of the nation's disposable income was spent on home improvements, new members of the family emerged to challenge the expertise of the wife and mother, the traditional arbiter of taste in the home. Very young children were now quick to denounce the most innocent purchases as *naff*. Of greater significance was the intervention by a new generation of men. Unlike their fathers, who would have been deemed odd in the extreme had they expressed strong views on home furnishings, this generation was eager to offer expert advice on the choice of everything from curtains to the kitchen kettle.

Our interviews with dozens of young couples point to a novel domestic power struggle centring on matters of taste. In practically all relationships where divisions over taste were apparent, women were trying to achieve a *comfortable* look in the home, while their menfolk were more concerned about its overall *statement*. Gender preferences seemed to be exacerbating their differences. Men were repeatedly seen to be impatient with overt displays of *femininity* and sentimentality. Dried flowers, floral designs, lace, cuddly toys and ornaments were all singled out as particular irritants deserving stiff resistance.

It's not stuff that run-of-the-mill people would have in their homes

Whatever private foibles are expressed by taste, it also functions as an important indicator of public status and class. Recent economic and social changes in Britain have led to a major upheaval of the nation's tastes.

Throughout the 80s a concentrated retailing and

marketing effort centred on the British home. During a period of apparent social mobility the British public required new choices to complement their changing social status, particularly as home-owners. Retailers obliged with a deluge of unfamiliar home paraphernalia, much of which was *antique* in design and inspired by a hotchpotch of historical fantasies: chiefly, the Country Cottage, the Farmhouse and the Stately Home. Nostalgia appears to hold a powerful grip on our national culture.

A great deal of evidence accumulated during the research for SIGNS OF THE TIMES tempts me to offer the following hypothesis: where you find rapid social mobility so you find a corresponding increase in anxiety about personal taste. The Thatcher years may have given the public new opportunities to define themselves through patterns of consumption rather than their social and educational background. However the flipside of this privilege was the vastly increased scope for *getting it wrong* in matters of taste. Mass retailers responded with sales techniques which left little to the imagination. They began to display fully furnished replica rooms, and stocked wide ranges of completely co-ordinated goods. At the more expensive end of the market, there was a boom in demand for interior designers. Many people's homes were about to look very different to their parents', and a good deal of help would be required to *get it right*.

Although retailers became increasingly adept at targeting and catering for highly specific categories of taste and *lifestyle*, this created a problem all of its own. As all-over styles such as Laura Ashley, Habitat and Next became widely and instantly identifiable, so their consumers incurred a potential loss of distinction and originality. In matters of taste there are few things more irritating than not being *a little bit different*. Worse still is the stigma of being regarded *predictable*.

When people are asked whether they are satisfied with the tastes they have selected, certain criteria are repeatedly invoked to explain or excuse their choices. These are most commonly: new v. old, exclusive v. common, expensive v. cheap, authentic v. artificial, and handcrafted v. mass produced. The motivations that underlie their choices appear equally polarised: Do I want to be the same as others or different? Should I go carefully or take risks? Should I be flamboyant or discreet?

I would like to think we have reasonably good taste, but we're not ostentatious or vulgar with it

The value placed upon discreet, inconspicuous or *effortless* taste, particularly by the professional classes, is significant for the almost impenetrable barrier it presents to the aspirant middle classes. Discreet taste conveys a confidence and an imperviousness to fashion which necessarily exclude those in the throes of arduous and conspicuous social advancement.

The distinction between conspicuous and discreet display provides some of the clearest possible evidence for the expression of rigid class difference through personal taste. On opposing sides of a London street, two houses face one another. One has expensive leaded windows in mock-Tudor style, a large carriage lamp and a front door with all manner of brass ornamentation. The other house is distinguished by its peeling paintwork, a carefully stripped pine door, and the oversized numerals 23 in the fan-light. The owners of the two households survey each other from close quarters and feel distinctly sorry for one another.

I remember very clearly when this carpet went down because it came over television that President Kennedy was assassinated

Whilst working on SIGNS OF THE TIMES, colleagues at the BBC were making films about important public issues such as homelessness, unemployment and Third World debt. When they enquired about our own endeavours, it was at times embarrassing to confess that we had spent the best part of 18 months talking to people about their choices of wallpaper and light fittings. At the end of this project, however, I am unrepentant about the subject of our research. Issues need not be *big* to contain important truths. The films and photographs which comprise SIGNS OF THE TIMES take as their agenda the banal details of personal taste in the home, and in my opinion the agenda is a timely one. After a decade of incessant discussion about fashion, style and design, it is strange how little attention has been paid to the innumerable ordinary decisions taken by people during the course of their daily lives. Discussion of taste was generally restricted to questions about marketing and people's relations with branded goods.

Apparently trivial matters of taste, when peered at carefully, reveal crucial expressions of private and social identity. As Martin Parr's photographs testify, they also say much about the exercise of domestic and cultural power in contemporary Britain.

NICHOLAS BARKER

Marie-Louise's pig irritates me intensely. I can't say why
but it just irritates me intensely

We are going to come to a nice compromise on every issue
I've already decided what colours we're going to have
He can just pick the variations

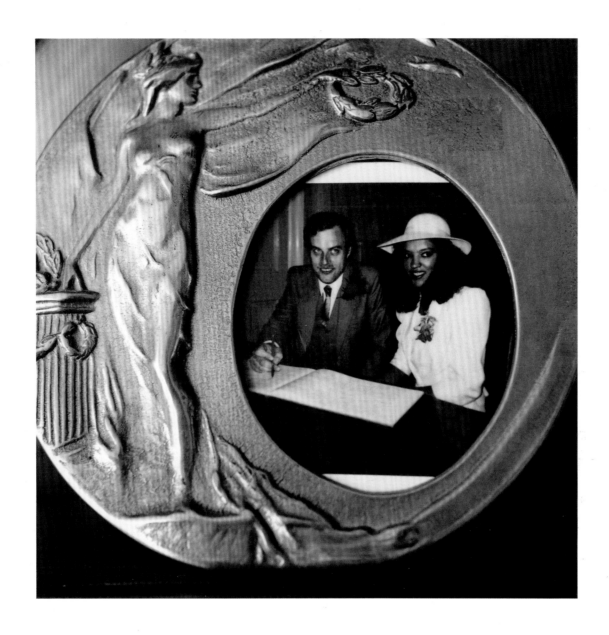

Alec has shown good taste once
– that was when he married me

It was very masculine when I came in here, so I put my
quilt out - the flowery one which he detests

They're ornaments, not toys
I don't play with them

After a few weeks living here I put out a few teddy bears
and he came home one day and just went mad about it

To come home in the evening to find the kids
have carried out their own form of anarchy
is just about the last thing I can face

You have to be very brave to live in a minimalist environment
Whenever people visit us I always feel I'm on show

Henry very much needs to be different. It's important
for him to live in a home that says Henry Harrison

I've only started showing an interest in the house since we got engaged. Before it was his house and his problem really

There wasn't anything here that had a feminine touch
I basically moved in and plonked things down

Sue has definitely given the bathroom the feminine touch

I spoke with Gary about the mug-tree but no
there was no way he would change it

I think we are looking for a look that is established
warm, comfortable, traditional

I'm put off real antiques because to me they look old
and sort of spooky

We wanted a cottagey
stately home kind of feel

There's nobody that's ever come in and said
'Oh I don't like the way you've got the place'

It is important I suppose to preserve
a little bit of old England

We thought we could make it look sort of bistro-y looking
in the kitchen and then carry it through into the lounge

Woodworm does generate through the furniture, and
obviously if you're putting new things into your home
the last thing you want is an invitation to worms

The fire has a light bulb underneath which we don't use
because it is very cheap looking

It's this Edwardian look that we're trying to achieve
from the bottom right up to the top of the house

Each to their own but I think this is going to be one of the best
– if not the best - houses on the estate

The trouble is, we do tend to be
dictated by fashion quite a lot

I think we are very lucky to have informed taste
– with my position as a fine arts valuer

You wouldn't get my daughter
to buy melamine

Anyone else would go to Bentalls and buy lace
Carol goes to Brighton

Dramatic, glamorous, over-the-top, I think
that's what we're looking for

I get such pleasure from them every
day when I sit in the bath

I don't think it's anything I particularly forced on Deborah
We've just always enjoyed the same sort of things

Underneath it all she really is a lovely girl

Mum's taste is boring. The only cool thing
in the sitting room is the parrot

She's basically turned her bedroom
into a hell hole

This is my clutter. This is me. Take it. If you don't like it
get out and that's your loss

Everything's got a memory to it, and getting rid of it
is like saying goodbye to the past

I never had a home of my own before
so it was time to really splurge out

When I looked at the wallpaper and the wallpaper looked at me
we instantly fell in love

I like to be surrounded by things that
are visually impressive

I am just one of those people that
likes to buy the latest gear

I wouldn't say it reflected me, no. It was more the way I
wanted it to look rather than a reflection of my personality

No, it took no courage at all. This was the way
I'd always wanted my bedroom to be

She's probably the most beautiful woman I've ever seen
It's unfortunate she's just a picture

It sounds boring, but I seem to spend a lot of time
just staring at the wall

Some men are a bit intimidated by my place. It's so
complete, and I really don't need a man's advice
as to how to make it any better

Everything's very important to me. I can't just live in an
ordinary house, it has to be a special house

We keep buying things thinking 'that'll look better'
and it just doesn't

I remember very clearly when this carpet went down
because it came over television that President
Kennedy was assassinated

But in the 1960s this was really tiptop fashion

It's not stuff that run-of-the-mill people would have
in their homes

Everything we've done is exclusive

I wanted to be a little bit different, a little bit individual
that's why I only did one side

Dimmers have made a big difference
you know, these days

We've got our foot on the ladder
that's basically what it's all about

It still feels as though we are living in a hotel suite. I want to
pick up the phone and ring for room service

The house came with everything
right down to the bars of soap

I would love to think I was the sort of person who
would have dried those flowers but I'm not
and I'm glad someone else has

I think we both feel we have got sufficient confidence to have
an idea about what we want to do, and do it properly

By and large I would always prefer to go to antique shops
and markets rather than to department stores

We recycle our bottles and newspapers but not our cans yet

I would like to think we have reasonably good taste
but we're not ostentatious or vulgar with it